MIDJOURNEY MASTERY: 1000+ PROMPT TEMPLATES

PREFACE

In the ever-evolving world of artificial intelligence, creativity, and innovation have found new avenues to flourish. MidJourney, a powerful AI bot on Discord, has emerged as a remarkable tool that allows users to generate stunning images using text prompts. It has opened doors to endless artistic possibilities, enabling both seasoned artists and novices to explore and create like never before.

"MidJourney Mastery - 1000+ Prompt Templates" is designed to be a comprehensive guide for anyone looking to master the art of using MidJourney. Whether you are just starting your journey or seeking to enhance your existing skills, this book offers valuable insights and guidance.

The first five chapters delve into the theory behind MidJourney, providing a solid foundation for understanding its commands, parameters, and functionalities. From basic commands to advanced image generation techniques, these chapters equip you with the knowledge to navigate MidJourney with confidence.

The heart of this book lies in the next twenty

chapters, each dedicated to prompt templates for different use cases. With over 1000 carefully crafted prompts, these chapters serve as a treasure trove of inspiration. They cover a wide array of themes, from nature and urban landscapes to technology, fashion, and beyond. Whether you are looking to create abstract art or depict historical scenes, you will find prompts that resonate with your creative vision.

"MidJourney Mastery - 1000+ Prompt Templates" is more than just a guide; it's a companion on your creative journey. It invites you to explore, experiment, and unleash your imagination. The prompts are not merely templates but sparks that can ignite your creativity.

As you embark on this exciting journey with MidJourney, may this book be your trusted guide, mentor, and source of inspiration. Happy image crafting!

CHAPTERS

1: INTRODUCTION TO MIDJOURNEY

Midjourney is a remarkable artificial intelligence (AI) bot that has taken the creative world by storm. Operating on Discord, it allows users to generate stunning images using simple text prompts. Whether you're an experienced artist or someone just starting to explore the world of visual creativity, Midjourney offers an accessible and innovative platform to unleash your imagination.

What is Midjourney?
At its core, Midjourney is a tool that translates text into visual art. By interacting with the Midjourney AI bot on Discord, users can create images, modify default settings, monitor user profiles, and perform several other helpful tasks. The primary command, /imagine, followed by a description, triggers the bot to create an image based on the given prompt.

How Does Midjourney Work?
Midjourney operates through a series of commands that users input on Discord. These commands range from basic ones like generating images to

more advanced parameters that modify the image generation process. Familiarizing yourself with these commands enhances your experience with Midjourney, allowing you to navigate and optimize your creative journey.

Why Use Midjourney?
Midjourney's appeal lies in its accessibility and innovation. It opens doors to artistic exploration without the need for advanced skills or expensive software. Whether you want to experiment with new styles, create abstract art, or depict specific scenes, Midjourney offers a platform to explore and create.

Getting Started with Midjourney
- Starting with Midjourney is a simple process.
- Download the discord app from https://discord.com.
- Open www.midjourney.com and you will find an option to add it to Discord.
- Create a server in the Discord app and add the MidJourney bot (which was already installed) to your server.

Begin by experimenting with basic commands and gradually explore the more advanced options. The community of Midjourney users on Discord also provides support and inspiration as you embark on your creative journey.

Midjourney represents a new era in creative

expression, bridging the gap between imagination and visual representation. It's more than just a tool; it's a companion on a creative journey filled with endless possibilities. As you delve deeper into this book, you'll uncover the full potential of Midjourney, from mastering commands to exploring prompt templates. Your journey into the world of AI-generated art has just begun, and the path ahead is filled with opportunities for discovery and creation.

2. MASTERING BASIC MIDJOURNEY COMMANDS

Midjourney offers a wide array of commands that enable users to create, modify, and explore visual art. Understanding these basic commands is the first step towards unlocking the full potential of Midjourney. This chapter provides an overview of the essential commands that every Midjourney user should know.

Understanding Commands

Commands in Midjourney are instructions given to the AI bot on Discord. By typing a specific command, users can trigger various actions, from generating images to toggling settings. Here's a look at some fundamental commands:

- **/ASK:** Get an answer to a question or blend two images together.
- **/DAILY_THEME:** Toggle notification pings for daily theme channel updates.
- **/DOCS:** Generate a link to topics covered in the Midjourney user guide.

- **/HELP:** Shows helpful information and tips about the Midjourney Bot.
- **/STEALTH:** For Pro Plan Subscribers, switch to Stealth Mode or Public Mode.

Image Generation with Text Prompts

The core functionality of Midjourney lies in generating images using text prompts. The command **/imagine** followed by a description will create an image based on the given text. Experimenting with different prompts allows users to explore various visual styles and concepts.

Example: /imagine A white cat playing with a ball in a park with greenery in the background.

Profile Monitoring and Settings Adjustment

Midjourney provides commands to monitor user information and adjust settings. Users can view their account details, queued or running jobs, and even switch between different modes like Fast mode or Relax mode.

Engaging with the Community

Midjourney's community on Discord is a vibrant space for collaboration and inspiration. Users can engage with others, share their creations, and learn from fellow Midjourney enthusiasts.

Deprecated and Extra Functionality Commands

Some commands have been replaced or deprecated, such as /private, which has been replaced with / stealth. Understanding these changes ensures a smooth user experience.

Mastering the basic commands of Midjourney is the foundation for a rewarding creative journey. These commands empower users to explore, create, and innovate, turning simple text into stunning visual art.

As you become more familiar with these commands, you'll be well-equipped to delve into the more advanced features and prompt templates that Midjourney offers. The path to creativity is at your fingertips, and the possibilities are endless.

3. ADVANCED PARAMETERS FOR IMAGE GENERATION

Building on the basic commands, Midjourney offers a range of advanced parameters that allow users to fine-tune their image generation process. These parameters provide greater control and customization, enabling users to create images that align with their specific vision and preferences.

Experimental Algorithms and Quality Control
Midjourney provides options to experiment with different algorithms and control the quality of the generated images. Users can specify parameters such as aspect ratios, width, height, and seed values to achieve the desired visual effects.

Artistic Styles and Image Quality
With Midjourney, users can explore various artistic styles and adjust the quality of the images. Parameters such as speed, detail, and cost considerations allow for a tailored creative experience. Whether you're aiming for a high-resolution masterpiece or a quick sketch,

Midjourney offers the flexibility to match your needs.

Modifying Midjourney Bot Settings

Beyond image generation, Midjourney provides commands to view and adjust the bot's settings. Users can create or manage custom options, specify suffixes for prompts, and toggle between different modes like Relax mode or Remix mode.

Generating Personal Links and Managing Jobs

Midjourney allows users to generate personal links for their account pages and manage their queued or running jobs. These functionalities provide a seamless user experience, making it easier to track and share your creative projects.

Switching Between Modes

For Pro Plan Subscribers, Midjourney offers the option to switch between Stealth Mode and Public Mode. These modes provide additional privacy and customization options, enhancing the overall user experience.

The advanced parameters for image generation in Midjourney open up a world of creative possibilities. By understanding and utilizing these parameters, users can take their creativity to new heights, crafting images that are not only visually stunning but also uniquely tailored to their vision. From experimenting with different styles to managing intricate details, Midjourney's advanced parameters empower users to explore and innovate without boundaries. The journey into the world of AI-generated art continues, and with these advanced tools at your disposal, the creative horizon is limitless.

4. STYLIZE AND QUALITY COMMANDS

Midjourney's capabilities extend beyond basic image generation, offering a suite of stylize and quality commands that allow users to craft images with precision and flair. This chapter delves into the various commands and options that enable users to enhance the style and quality of their creations.

Exploring Artistic Styles

Midjourney provides a range of artistic styles that users can apply to their images. From abstract and surreal to realistic and detailed, these styles offer a diverse palette to suit different creative tastes. Experimenting with these styles can lead to unexpected and inspiring results.

Controlling Image Quality

Quality is a crucial aspect of any visual creation, and Midjourney offers commands to control the resolution, detail, and overall quality of the generated images. Whether you're aiming for a high-definition masterpiece or a stylized sketch, these commands provide the flexibility to achieve your desired outcome.

Speed, Detail, and Cost Considerations

Midjourney allows users to balance speed, detail, and cost when generating images. By adjusting these parameters, users can optimize the image generation process to fit their needs and preferences. Whether you prioritize speed for quick previews or detail for the final product, Midjourney offers the control to make it happen.

Experimenting with Different Modes

Midjourney offers various modes such as Fast mode, Relax mode, and Remix mode. These modes provide different experiences and outcomes, allowing users to explore and find the approach that best fits their creative process.

Custom Options and Personalization

With Midjourney, creativity knows no bounds. Users can create and manage custom options, specify suffixes for prompts, and even regenerate jobs within Discord using specific IDs. These functionalities provide a personalized and seamless creative experience.

Stylize and quality commands in Midjourney are essential tools for any creator looking to elevate their visual art. These commands offer a rich and diverse set of options to explore, experiment, and perfect your creations. From artistic styles to quality control, Midjourney empowers users to craft images that resonate with their vision and creativity. The journey with Midjourney is filled with endless possibilities, and with these tools at your fingertips, the path to artistic mastery awaits.

5: PREFERENCES, SETTINGS, AND ADDITIONAL COMMANDS

Midjourney's versatility extends to its wide array of preferences, settings, and additional commands that provide users with a tailored and efficient creative experience. This chapter explores these aspects, offering insights into how users can customize their interaction with Midjourney to align with their unique needs and preferences.

Modifying Midjourney Bot Settings

Midjourney allows users to view and adjust the bot's settings, providing control over various aspects of the user experience.

- **Photo Types:** Users can specify the type of photo they want, such as vector, natural, or cartoon.(Just mention at the end of the prompt)
- **Aspect Resolutions:** Midjourney supports different aspect ratios like 16:9, 4:3, or 1:1, allowing users to create images that fit specific

dimensions. (Just mention at the end of the prompt, ex: ar 16:9 for thumbnail)

- **Notification Preferences:** Toggle notification pings for daily theme channel updates or other notifications.

Creating and Managing Custom Options

Custom options in Midjourney enable users to define specific parameters that can be applied to their prompts.

- Quality Settings: Define the quality of the generated image, ranging from low to high resolution.
- Style Preferences: Apply specific styles such as abstract, realistic, or sketch to achieve desired visual effects.

Specifying Suffixes and Regenerating Jobs

- **Suffixes:** Specify a suffix to add to the end of every prompt, allowing for consistent tagging or categorization.
- **Regenerating Jobs:** Use an image's Job ID to regenerate the job within Discord, providing flexibility in managing and revisiting past creations.

Switching Between Modes and Other Functionalities

- **Stealth Mode and Public Mode:** Switch between private and public modes to control the visibility of your creations.

- **Relax Mode and Remix Mode:** Explore different creative approaches with these specialized modes.

Preferences, settings, and additional commands in Midjourney provide a rich and customizable creative experience. From specifying photo types and aspect resolutions to fine-tuning settings and exploring different modes, these aspects empower users to craft a Midjourney experience that resonates with their creative vision and workflow. As you continue to explore and create with Midjourney, these tools and options will serve as valuable companions, enhancing your journey and unlocking new horizons of creativity.

6. PROMPT TEMPLATES FOR NATURE IMAGERY

Nature has always been a profound source of inspiration for artists, and Midjourney offers an exciting platform to explore and create nature-themed images. This chapter provides a collection of prompt templates that can be used to generate stunning visuals of landscapes, flora, fauna, and other natural elements.

Landscapes

1. /imagine A majestic mountain range at sunrise
2. /imagine Turquoise ocean waves crashing against a rocky shore
3. /imagine Sweeping sand dunes under a scorching sun
4. /imagine A tranquil forest with sunlight filtering through the leaves
5. /imagine A serene lake reflecting the colors of a sunset
6. /imagine A winding river cutting through a

lush valley

7. /imagine A glacier slowly moving through a frozen landscape
8. /imagine A waterfall cascading down a steep cliff
9. /imagine Rolling hills covered in wildflowers
10. /imagine A dense jungle filled with exotic plants

Flora

1. /imagine A field of vibrant flowers in full bloom
2. /imagine An ancient tree with gnarled branches and deep roots
3. /imagine Lush tropical plants with colorful flowers and exotic fruits
4. /imagine A tree shedding its golden autumn leaves
5. /imagine A delicate orchid growing in a rainforest
6. /imagine A cactus garden thriving in the desert
7. /imagine A vine-covered archway leading to a secret garden
8. /imagine A cherry blossom tree in full bloom
9. /imagine A sunflower field stretching to the horizon
10. /imagine A moss-covered forest floor

Fauna

1. /imagine A group of elephants roaming the African savannah
2. /imagine A flock of birds taking flight at sunset
3. /imagine A colorful coral reef teeming with marine life
4. /imagine A delicate butterfly perched on a blooming flower
5. /imagine A family of deer grazing in a meadow
6. /imagine A school of fish swimming in crystal clear water
7. /imagine A majestic eagle soaring through the sky
8. /imagine A playful dolphin jumping out of the ocean
9. /imagine A wise owl perched on a tree branch
10. /imagine A spider weaving its intricate web

Weather and Atmosphere

1. /imagine A dramatic thunderstorm with lightning striking the ground
2. /imagine A serene snowy landscape with snowflakes gently falling
3. /imagine A bright rainbow arching across the sky after a rain shower
4. /imagine A clear starry night with a glowing full moon

5. /imagine A foggy morning in a mountain valley
6. /imagine A tornado forming over a flat plain
7. /imagine A hailstorm pounding against a rugged landscape
8. /imagine A hurricane viewed from space
9. /imagine A gentle breeze rustling the leaves of a forest
10. /imagine A heatwave shimmering over a desert

Miscellaneous Nature Themes

1. /imagine A volcanic eruption with lava flowing down the mountain
2. /imagine An ice cave illuminated by a soft blue light
3. /imagine A geothermal hot spring surrounded by snow
4. /imagine A meteor shower lighting up the night sky
5. /imagine A rock formation shaped by centuries of erosion
6. /imagine A forest recovering after a wildfire
7. /imagine A swamp filled with diverse wildlife
8. /imagine An oasis in the middle of a desert
9. /imagine A secluded beach with white sand and clear water
10. /imagine A path leading through a dense

forest to a hidden waterfall

Feel free to modify and experiment with these templates to create your unique interpretations of nature's splendor. Happy creating!

7. PROMPT TEMPLATES FOR URBAN LANDSCAPES

Urban landscapes offer a rich tapestry of architectural marvels, bustling streets, iconic landmarks, and diverse cityscapes. This chapter provides 50 prompt templates to explore and create images that capture the essence of urban life and landscapes.

1. /imagine A bustling city street with neon signs at night
2. /imagine A historic town square with a grand clock tower
3. /imagine A modern skyscraper reflecting the blue sky
4. /imagine A narrow alleyway filled with street art
5. /imagine A rooftop garden overlooking the city skyline
6. /imagine A crowded subway station during rush hour
7. /imagine A tranquil city park with a pond and bridge

8. /imagine A lively outdoor market with colorful stalls

9. /imagine A futuristic cityscape with flying cars

10. /imagine A historic bridge spanning a wide river in the city

11. /imagine A cityscape view from a high vantage point at sunset

12. /imagine A cobblestone street lined with quaint cafes

13. /imagine A city street after a rain shower with reflections

14. /imagine A grand city entrance gate with ornate details

15. /imagine A city harbor filled with boats and ships

16. /imagine A bustling airport terminal with travelers

17. /imagine A city's financial district with towering buildings

18. /imagine A lively street festival with music and dance

19. /imagine A quiet residential street with brownstone houses

20. /imagine A cityscape silhouette against a fiery sunset

21. /imagine A modern shopping mall with glass architecture

22. /imagine A city street filled with cherry blossom trees

23. /imagine A historic castle in the heart of a

city

24. /imagine A city's cultural district with theaters and museums

25. /imagine A city square with a grand fountain centerpiece

26. /imagine A city's industrial area with factories and warehouses

27. /imagine A city's waterfront promenade with benches

28. /imagine A city's old town with preserved architecture

29. /imagine A city's university campus with students

30. /imagine A city's central train station with platforms

31. /imagine A city's sports stadium filled with fans

32. /imagine A city's beachfront with palm trees and cafes

33. /imagine A city's government district with official buildings

34. /imagine A city's zoo with families enjoying the day

35. /imagine A city's amusement park with roller coasters

36. /imagine A city's library with grand columns and steps

37. /imagine A city's hospital complex with helipad

38. /imagine A city's fire station with red fire trucks

39. /imagine A city's police station with patrol cars

40. /imagine A city's school building with children playing

41. /imagine A city's cemetery with historic gravestones

42. /imagine A city's art gallery with modern design

43. /imagine A city's science museum with interactive exhibits

44. /imagine A city's botanical garden with exotic plants

45. /imagine A city's aquarium with marine life displays

46. /imagine A city's observatory with telescopes

47. /imagine A city's spa and wellness center

48. /imagine A city's luxury hotel with a grand lobby

49. /imagine A city's recycling center with sustainability features

50. /imagine A city's tech hub with innovative startups

These prompts offer a diverse exploration of urban landscapes, capturing the vibrancy, architecture, culture, and daily life of cities. Feel free to modify and experiment with these templates to create your unique interpretations of urban scenes. Happy creating!

8. PROMPT TEMPLATES FOR CHARACTER DESIGN

Character design is a fascinating aspect of visual storytelling, encompassing everything from humans to mythical creatures. This chapter provides 50 prompt templates to inspire and guide the creation of diverse and unique characters.

1. /imagine A heroic knight in shining armor
2. /imagine A mysterious sorceress casting a spell
3. /imagine A futuristic robot with human-like features
4. /imagine A wise old wizard with a magical staff
5. /imagine A cunning thief sneaking in the shadows
6. /imagine A brave astronaut exploring alien worlds
7. /imagine A gentle forest nymph surrounded by nature
8. /imagine A fierce warrior from an ancient tribe

9. /imagine A charismatic pirate captain with a parrot

10. /imagine A whimsical fairy with delicate wings

11. /imagine A determined detective with a magnifying glass

12. /imagine A loving grandmother knitting by the fire

13. /imagine A mischievous child with a slingshot

14. /imagine A noble queen wearing a jeweled crown

15. /imagine A mad scientist in a cluttered laboratory

16. /imagine A graceful ballerina performing on stage

17. /imagine A rugged cowboy riding a wild horse

18. /imagine A fearless firefighter battling flames

19. /imagine A talented chef creating a culinary masterpiece

20. /imagine A caring nurse tending to a patient

21. /imagine A diligent farmer working in the fields

22. /imagine A cheerful clown entertaining at a circus

23. /imagine A wise sensei teaching martial arts

24. /imagine A skilled archer aiming a bow and

arrow

25. /imagine A mystical mermaid singing by the sea

26. /imagine A relentless zombie on the prowl

27. /imagine A gentle giant protecting a village

28. /imagine A curious alien exploring Earth

29. /imagine A legendary dragon guarding treasure

30. /imagine A playful ghost haunting an old mansion

31. /imagine A resourceful inventor with gadgets

32. /imagine A regal emperor in ceremonial robes

33. /imagine A daring explorer in a jungle

34. /imagine A loyal dog waiting for its owner

35. /imagine A graceful swan transforming into a princess

36. /imagine A powerful superhero in dynamic pose

37. /imagine A sinister villain plotting revenge

38. /imagine A wise oracle foreseeing the future

39. /imagine A charming prince searching for love

40. /imagine A rebellious teenager with a skateboard

41. /imagine A serene monk meditating in peace

42. /imagine A joyful musician playing a guitar
43. /imagine A protective father holding a baby
44. /imagine A fearless journalist uncovering truth
45. /imagine A skilled pilot navigating through storms
46. /imagine A compassionate teacher inspiring students
47. /imagine A diligent construction worker building
48. /imagine A graceful model walking the runway
49. /imagine A friendly shopkeeper in a small store
50. /imagine A dedicated athlete training for victory

These prompts offer a wide range of character design possibilities, from everyday people to fantastical beings. Feel free to modify and experiment with these templates to create characters that resonate with your stories and visions. Happy creating!

9. PROMPT TEMPLATES FOR ABSTRACT ART

Abstract art opens up a world of imagination, emotion, and experimentation. It allows for the expression of ideas and feelings that may not be easily represented in traditional forms. This chapter provides 50 prompt templates to inspire and guide the creation of abstract art pieces.

1. /imagine A dance of colors and shapes in a rhythmic pattern
2. /imagine A chaotic explosion of geometric forms
3. /imagine A serene landscape of soft, blended hues
4. /imagine A bold contrast of black and white lines
5. /imagine A fluid motion of watercolor splashes
6. /imagine A complex maze of intertwined spirals
7. /imagine A delicate balance of light and shadow

8. /imagine A vibrant energy radiating from the center
9. /imagine A fragmented reflection in broken mirrors
10. /imagine A dreamlike swirl of clouds and stars
11. /imagine A harmonious blend of warm and cool tones
12. /imagine A pulsating rhythm of concentric circles
13. /imagine A visual echo of sound waves
14. /imagine A playful interaction of primary colors
15. /imagine A mysterious depth of layered textures
16. /imagine A surreal fusion of organic and mechanical
17. /imagine A symbolic representation of time's passage
18. /imagine A minimalist composition of simple shapes
19. /imagine A dynamic tension between opposites
20. /imagine A poetic flow of calligraphic lines
21. /imagine A visual metaphor for growth and transformation
22. /imagine A chaotic dance of particles and waves
23. /imagine A meditative pattern of repeating elements
24. /imagine A bold statement with

monochromatic shades

25. /imagine A whimsical journey through an imaginary landscape
26. /imagine A tactile exploration of rough and smooth surfaces
27. /imagine A celebration of diversity through varied forms
28. /imagine A visual harmony of complementary colors
29. /imagine A symbolic bridge connecting two realms
30. /imagine A fragmented reality seen through prisms
31. /imagine A cosmic exploration of space and dimension
32. /imagine A gentle embrace of curved and flowing lines
33. /imagine A stark contrast of organic and geometric shapes
34. /imagine A rhythmic pattern of dots and dashes
35. /imagine A visual poem of texture and tone
36. /imagine A conceptual representation of human emotion
37. /imagine A vibrant dance of light and movement
38. /imagine A tranquil meditation on symmetry and balance
39. /imagine A bold exploration of scale and perspective

40. /imagine A playful interaction of positive and negative space
41. /imagine A dynamic collision of order and chaos
42. /imagine A reflective journey through layered transparency
43. /imagine A visual symphony of harmonious discord
44. /imagine A tactile sensation of embossed patterns
45. /imagine A whimsical flight of floating shapes
46. /imagine A surreal landscape of melting forms
47. /imagine A visual echo of nature's fractal patterns
48. /imagine A conceptual map of interconnected ideas
49. /imagine A symbolic fusion of past, present, and future
50. /imagine A visual meditation on solitude and connection

These prompts offer a diverse exploration of abstract art, capturing various themes, emotions, and visual experiments. Feel free to modify and experiment with these templates to create abstract pieces that resonate with your artistic vision. Happy creating!

10. PROMPT TEMPLATES FOR HISTORICAL SCENES

Historical scenes provide a window into the past, allowing us to visualize significant moments, cultures, events, and figures. This chapter provides 50 prompt templates to inspire and guide the creation of art that captures various historical epochs and themes.

1. /imagine A bustling medieval market square
2. /imagine A grand Roman amphitheater with gladiators
3. /imagine A solemn signing of a historic treaty
4. /imagine A majestic Egyptian pyramid under construction
5. /imagine A lively Renaissance art studio
6. /imagine A dramatic Viking ship sailing stormy seas
7. /imagine A solemn samurai duel under cherry blossoms
8. /imagine A grand Victorian ballroom dance

9. /imagine A tense American Revolutionary War battle

10. /imagine A vibrant Native American tribal ceremony

11. /imagine A historic moon landing by astronauts

12. /imagine A bustling Industrial Revolution factory

13. /imagine A serene ancient Greek philosopher's garden

14. /imagine A lively Wild West saloon scene

15. /imagine A solemn Civil Rights march in the 1960s

16. /imagine A grand inauguration of the Panama Canal

17. /imagine A dramatic sinking of the Titanic

18. /imagine A vibrant Harlem Renaissance jazz club

19. /imagine A tense Berlin Wall escape attempt

20. /imagine A bustling ancient Chinese Silk Road market

21. /imagine A grand Aztec temple ceremony

22. /imagine A dramatic French Revolution guillotine scene

23. /imagine A solemn World War I trench warfare

24. /imagine A lively 1920s flapper dance party

25. /imagine A historic Wright brothers' first flight

26. /imagine A grand ancient Babylonian

hanging garden

27. /imagine A dramatic Christopher Columbus' landing

28. /imagine A vibrant Mardi Gras parade in early New Orleans

29. /imagine A tense Cuban Missile Crisis negotiation

30. /imagine A solemn ancient Druid ceremony at Stonehenge

31. /imagine A bustling Gold Rush town in California

32. /imagine A grand coronation of a British monarch

33. /imagine A dramatic storming of the Bastille

34. /imagine A vibrant ancient Indian festival of colors

35. /imagine A solemn funeral procession for a Pharaoh

36. /imagine A lively Prohibition-era speakeasy

37. /imagine A dramatic rescue on the Underground Railroad

38. /imagine A grand Ottoman Empire court scene

39. /imagine A vibrant 1950s American diner scene

40. /imagine A solemn signing of the Magna Carta

41. /imagine A bustling ancient Mesopotamian city

42. /imagine A dramatic Marco Polo's journey on the Silk Road
43. /imagine A vibrant Venetian Carnival in the Renaissance
44. /imagine A solemn fall of the Berlin Wall
45. /imagine A dramatic ancient Spartan battle scene
46. /imagine A grand Ming Dynasty imperial court
47. /imagine A vibrant Roaring Twenties street scene
48. /imagine A solemn Nelson Mandela's release from prison
49. /imagine A grand ancient Mayan astronomical observatory
50. /imagine A lively colonial Boston Tea Party

These prompts offer a diverse exploration of historical scenes, capturing various eras, cultures, events, and figures. Feel free to modify and experiment with these templates to create historical pieces that resonate with your interest in the past. Happy creating!

11. PROMPT TEMPLATES FOR FUTURISTIC CONCEPTS

Futuristic concepts allow us to explore the unknown, envisioning technology, societies, landscapes, and possibilities that lie ahead. This chapter provides 50 prompt templates to inspire and guide the creation of art that captures various futuristic themes and ideas.

1. /imagine A bustling futuristic cityscape with flying cars
2. /imagine A high-tech space station orbiting Earth
3. /imagine A robotic factory with autonomous machines
4. /imagine A virtual reality classroom with holographic lessons
5. /imagine A futuristic medical lab with advanced diagnostics
6. /imagine A desert colony on Mars with biodomes

7. /imagine A high-speed magnetic levitation train
8. /imagine A deep-sea exploration vessel with AI crew
9. /imagine A cybernetic human with integrated technology
10. /imagine A renewable energy farm with solar and wind power
11. /imagine A spaceport with interstellar travel capabilities
12. /imagine A futuristic fashion show with smart fabrics
13. /imagine A smart city with interconnected IoT devices
14. /imagine A post-apocalyptic landscape with survivors
15. /imagine A futuristic library with digital knowledge access
16. /imagine A space battle with advanced fighter ships
17. /imagine A time-travel portal with temporal explorers
18. /imagine A futuristic concert with holographic performers
19. /imagine A drone delivery network in a busy city
20. /imagine A climate-controlled indoor agricultural farm
21. /imagine A futuristic courtroom with AI judges
22. /imagine A space exploration mission to

distant galaxies

23. /imagine A high-tech fitness center with virtual trainers

24. /imagine A futuristic family home with automation

25. /imagine A space tourism resort on the Moon

26. /imagine A futuristic art gallery with interactive exhibits

27. /imagine A self-driving car highway with smart traffic

28. /imagine A futuristic zoo with virtual animal encounters

29. /imagine A space colony on a distant exoplanet

30. /imagine A futuristic underwater city with domes

31. /imagine A high-tech military base with robotic soldiers

32. /imagine A futuristic amusement park with VR rides

33. /imagine A space elevator connecting Earth to orbit

34. /imagine A futuristic archaeological dig with drones

35. /imagine A high-tech recycling center with zero waste

36. /imagine A futuristic shopping mall with AI assistants

37. /imagine A space observatory studying black holes

38. /imagine A futuristic emergency response with drones
39. /imagine A high-tech police force with cybernetic enhancements
40. /imagine A futuristic spa with rejuvenation therapies
41. /imagine A space mining operation on an asteroid
42. /imagine A futuristic school with personalized learning
43. /imagine A high-tech election with secure online voting
44. /imagine A futuristic retirement community in space
45. /imagine A high-tech weather control station
46. /imagine A futuristic film studio with AI directors
47. /imagine A space research lab with alien specimens
48. /imagine A futuristic bank with cryptocurrency
49. /imagine A high-tech construction site with 3D printing
50. /imagine A futuristic theme park with robotic mascots

These prompts offer a diverse exploration of futuristic concepts, capturing various themes, technologies, and visions of what may lie ahead. Feel free to modify and experiment with these templates to create futuristic pieces that resonate with your imagination and curiosity. Happy creating!

12. PROMPT TEMPLATES FOR EMOTIONAL THEMES

Emotional themes allow us to explore and express the vast spectrum of human feelings and experiences. This chapter provides 50 prompt templates to inspire and guide the creation of art that captures various emotional states and moments.

1. /imagine A joyful celebration with fireworks and laughter
2. /imagine A sorrowful farewell at a train station
3. /imagine A peaceful meditation by a tranquil lake
4. /imagine A passionate embrace between lovers
5. /imagine A fearful encounter with a shadowy figure
6. /imagine A hopeful sunrise over a new beginning
7. /imagine A nostalgic walk down a childhood street

8. /imagine A courageous stand against overwhelming odds
9. /imagine A confused maze with no clear path
10. /imagine A surprised birthday party with friends
11. /imagine A lonely night under a starlit sky
12. /imagine A determined climb up a steep mountain
13. /imagine A playful dance in a field of flowers
14. /imagine A jealous glance at a rival's success
15. /imagine A comforting hug during a time of loss
16. /imagine A curious exploration of a mysterious forest
17. /imagine A proud graduation day with family
18. /imagine A relaxing vacation on a tropical beach
19. /imagine A frustrated attempt to solve a puzzle
20. /imagine A triumphant victory on the sports field
21. /imagine A romantic dinner under the moonlight
22. /imagine A heartbroken farewell at a graveside
23. /imagine A contented evening by a warm fireplace
24. /imagine A rebellious act of defiance

25. /imagine A grateful embrace of a helpful friend
26. /imagine A suspenseful chase through dark alleys
27. /imagine A compassionate act of kindness to a stranger
28. /imagine A regretful look back at a missed opportunity
29. /imagine A faithful vigil by a loved one's bedside
30. /imagine A humorous mishap at a family gathering
31. /imagine A serene moment of reflection in a garden
32. /imagine A triumphant return home after a long journey
33. /imagine A loving family reunion after years apart
34. /imagine A restless night filled with worry
35. /imagine A joyful discovery of a hidden talent
36. /imagine A sorrowful memory of a lost love
37. /imagine A peaceful resolution to a conflict
38. /imagine A passionate pursuit of a creative dream
39. /imagine A fearful anticipation of an upcoming event
40. /imagine A hopeful planting of a new tree
41. /imagine A nostalgic visit to an old school

42. /imagine A courageous rescue in a storm
43. /imagine A playful splash in a summer pool
44. /imagine A jealous guarding of a treasured possession
45. /imagine A comforting lullaby to a child
46. /imagine A curious investigation of a hidden door
47. /imagine A proud display of a personal achievement
48. /imagine A relaxing soak in a hot spring
49. /imagine A frustrated struggle with a stubborn problem
50. /imagine A triumphant completion of a challenging project

These prompts offer a diverse exploration of emotional themes, capturing various feelings, experiences, and moments that resonate with the human condition. Feel free to modify and experiment with these templates to create emotional pieces that speak to your heart and soul. Happy creating!

13. PROMPT TEMPLATES FOR SEASONAL IMAGERY

Seasonal imagery allows us to explore and celebrate the changing cycles of nature, each with its unique beauty, symbolism, and emotions. This chapter provides 50 prompt templates to inspire and guide the creation of art that captures various seasonal themes and moments.

Spring

1. /imagine A vibrant field of blooming tulips in spring
2. /imagine A gentle spring rain nourishing new growth
3. /imagine A joyful spring festival with colorful kites
4. /imagine A peaceful spring morning with singing birds
5. /imagine A romantic cherry blossom walk in spring

Summer

1. /imagine A lively summer beach party with friends
2. /imagine A relaxing summer hammock nap under palm trees
3. /imagine A thrilling summer hike on a mountain trail
4. /imagine A refreshing summer splash in a clear lake
5. /imagine A vibrant summer sunset over the ocean

Autumn

1. /imagine A cozy autumn evening by a crackling fire
2. /imagine A scenic autumn drive through colorful foliage
3. /imagine A peaceful autumn harvest with pumpkins and corn
4. /imagine A nostalgic autumn walk through a leaf-strewn path
5. /imagine A festive autumn fair with hayrides and cider

Winter

1. /imagine A magical winter wonderland with sparkling snow
2. /imagine A joyful winter ice skating rink with laughter
3. /imagine A cozy winter cabin with warm blankets

4. /imagine A festive winter holiday market with twinkling lights
5. /imagine A serene winter night with falling snowflakes

Multi-Seasonal

1. /imagine A tree through all four seasons in a time-lapse
2. /imagine A seasonal garden growing and changing over a year
3. /imagine A seasonal feast with dishes from spring to winter
4. /imagine A seasonal fashion show with styles for all seasons
5. /imagine A seasonal migration of birds across continents

Specific Seasonal Events

1. /imagine A lively spring Easter egg hunt
2. /imagine A thrilling summer solstice celebration
3. /imagine A spooky autumn Halloween night
4. /imagine A joyful winter Christmas morning
5. /imagine A festive New Year's Eve countdown in winter

Seasonal Activities

1. /imagine Planting flowers in a spring garden

2. /imagine Building sandcastles on a summer beach
3. /imagine Picking apples in an autumn orchard
4. /imagine Skiing down a snowy winter mountain
5. /imagine Fishing on a tranquil summer lake

Seasonal Symbolism

1. /imagine Spring as a rebirth with butterflies and buds
2. /imagine Summer as a time of abundance with sunflowers
3. /imagine Autumn as a time of reflection with falling leaves
4. /imagine Winter as a time of rest with a hibernating bear

Seasonal Weather

1. /imagine A spring thunderstorm with lightning
2. /imagine A hot summer day with a blazing sun
3. /imagine A misty autumn morning with dew
4. /imagine A chilly winter day with icicles

Seasonal Foods

1. /imagine A spring picnic with fresh salads
2. /imagine A summer barbecue with grilled

meats

3. /imagine An autumn feast with roasted vegetables
4. /imagine A winter meal with hearty soups

Seasonal Wildlife

1. /imagine Spring lambs frolicking in a meadow
2. /imagine Summer fireflies glowing at dusk
3. /imagine Winter penguins huddling for warmth

These prompts offer a diverse exploration of seasonal imagery, capturing the essence, activities, and beauty of each season. Feel free to modify and experiment with these templates to create seasonal pieces that resonate with your appreciation for nature's cycles. Happy creating!

14. PROMPT TEMPLATES FOR CULTURAL REPRESENTATIONS

Cultural representations allow us to explore, celebrate, and honor the rich diversity of human traditions, customs, beliefs, and expressions. This chapter provides 50 prompt templates to inspire and guide the creation of art that captures various cultural themes and elements.

1. /imagine A lively Brazilian Carnival parade with dancers
2. /imagine A traditional Japanese tea ceremony
3. /imagine A vibrant Indian Holi festival with colorful powders
4. /imagine A solemn Native American tribal dance
5. /imagine A festive Mexican Day of the Dead celebration
6. /imagine A traditional Chinese dragon dance

7. /imagine A historic Scottish Highland Games competition
8. /imagine A graceful Polynesian hula dance
9. /imagine A lively Irish St. Patrick's Day parade
10. /imagine A traditional African drumming circle
11. /imagine A festive Italian Venetian Carnival masquerade
12. /imagine A solemn Jewish Hanukkah menorah lighting
13. /imagine A vibrant Spanish Flamenco dance performance
14. /imagine A traditional Russian Matryoshka doll crafting
15. /imagine A festive Canadian Thanksgiving family meal
16. /imagine A historic Greek Olympic Games scene
17. /imagine A traditional Maori haka war dance
18. /imagine A lively Turkish Whirling Dervish ceremony
19. /imagine A festive German Oktoberfest celebration
20. /imagine A traditional Korean Hanbok dress fitting
21. /imagine A solemn Islamic call to prayer in a mosque
22. /imagine A vibrant Mardi Gras parade in New Orleans

23. /imagine A traditional Thai water festival celebration
24. /imagine A historic Viking ship sailing with warriors
25. /imagine A traditional Ethiopian coffee ceremony
26. /imagine A festive Dutch Tulip Festival with windmills
27. /imagine A traditional Hawaiian luau feast
28. /imagine A solemn Tibetan Buddhist meditation
29. /imagine A lively Colombian salsa dance performance
30. /imagine A traditional Swedish Midsummer celebration
31. /imagine A historic Roman gladiator fight in the Colosseum
32. /imagine A traditional Vietnamese water puppet show
33. /imagine A festive Australian Christmas barbecue on the beach
34. /imagine A traditional Moroccan market with spices
35. /imagine A lively English Morris dance performance
36. /imagine A traditional Peruvian alpaca wool weaving
37. /imagine A festive Filipino Ati-Atihan festival dance
38. /imagine A traditional Swiss yodeling

performance

39. /imagine A historic Egyptian Pharaoh's coronation

40. /imagine A traditional French wine harvest celebration

41. /imagine A lively Jamaican reggae music festival

42. /imagine A traditional Nepali Tihar festival of lights

43. /imagine A festive Hungarian folk dance performance

44. /imagine A traditional Chilean rodeo competition

45. /imagine A solemn Armenian khachkar stone carving

46. /imagine A vibrant Cuban street music performance

47. /imagine A traditional Jordanian Bedouin desert feast

48. /imagine A festive Belgian chocolate festival

49. /imagine A traditional Saudi Arabian camel race

50. /imagine A lively South African Zulu dance performance

These prompts offer a diverse exploration of cultural representations, capturing various traditions, customs, celebrations, and expressions from around the world. Feel free to modify and experiment with these templates to create cultural pieces that resonate with your appreciation for human diversity and creativity. Happy creating!

15. PROMPT TEMPLATES FOR SPACE AND ASTRONOMY

Space and astronomy open up a universe of possibilities, allowing us to explore celestial bodies, cosmic phenomena, and the mysteries of the cosmos. This chapter provides 50 prompt templates to inspire and guide the creation of art that captures various space and astronomical themes.

1. /imagine A breathtaking view of Earth from the Moon's surface
2. /imagine A vibrant Milky Way galaxy as seen from a dark sky
3. /imagine A futuristic space colony on Mars
4. /imagine A majestic solar eclipse with a glowing corona
5. /imagine A lively meteor shower streaking across the night sky
6. /imagine A mysterious black hole devouring a star
7. /imagine A serene spacewalk outside the

International Space Station

8. /imagine A colorful nebula forming new stars
9. /imagine A historic Apollo moon landing scene
10. /imagine A futuristic spaceport with interstellar travel
11. /imagine A close-up view of Saturn's rings
12. /imagine A thrilling space battle with futuristic spacecraft
13. /imagine A peaceful alien planet with exotic flora and fauna
14. /imagine A detailed surface exploration of Jupiter's moon Europa
15. /imagine A grand space telescope observing distant galaxies
16. /imagine A mysterious wormhole connecting two points in space
17. /imagine A lively astronaut training session at a space camp
18. /imagine A stunning aurora borealis over a snowy landscape
19. /imagine A dramatic supernova explosion in a distant galaxy
20. /imagine A futuristic space elevator connecting Earth to orbit
21. /imagine A detailed study of the Sun's surface with solar flares
22. /imagine A peaceful space meditation in zero gravity
23. /imagine A thrilling asteroid mining

operation

24. /imagine A mysterious encounter with an alien civilization

25. /imagine A grand observatory with a giant telescope

26. /imagine A serene cosmic ballet of binary stars

27. /imagine A futuristic space tourism resort on the Moon

28. /imagine A detailed map of the constellations in the night sky

29. /imagine A historic space mission control during a launch

30. /imagine A thrilling journey through a cosmic dust storm

31. /imagine A peaceful space garden growing food in zero gravity

32. /imagine A mysterious radio signal from a distant star

33. /imagine A grand cosmic alignment of planets in the solar system

34. /imagine A futuristic space race with advanced technology

35. /imagine A detailed exploration of an asteroid's surface

36. /imagine A grand celebration of human settlement on another planet

37. /imagine A mysterious cosmic event creating a new star

38. /imagine A thrilling rescue mission in deep space

39. /imagine A peaceful contemplation of the universe's vastness
40. /imagine A lively space-themed amusement park on Earth
41. /imagine A detailed scientific analysis of a comet's composition
42. /imagine A grand space opera performance in a cosmic theater
43. /imagine A futuristic space habitat with artificial gravity
44. /imagine A thrilling space exploration video game adventure
45. /imagine A peaceful cosmic meditation with celestial sounds
46. /imagine A grand space museum with historic artifacts
47. /imagine A mysterious cosmic anomaly defying explanation
48. /imagine A futuristic space fashion show with zero-gravity designs
49. /imagine A thrilling space expedition to a distant galaxy
50. /imagine A peaceful cosmic journey through the universe in a dream

These prompts offer a diverse exploration of space and astronomical themes, capturing various celestial phenomena, cosmic wonders, and futuristic space concepts. Feel free to modify and experiment with these templates to create space-themed pieces that resonate with your curiosity and fascination with the universe. Happy creating!

16. PROMPT TEMPLATES FOR FANTASY WORLDS

Fantasy worlds allow us to explore realms of imagination, magic, mythical creatures, and extraordinary landscapes. This chapter provides 50 prompt templates to inspire and guide the creation of art that captures various fantasy themes and elements.

1. /imagine A majestic castle floating on a cloud
2. /imagine A mystical forest filled with glowing fairies
3. /imagine A fierce battle between dragons and knights
4. /imagine A magical library with books that come to life
5. /imagine A hidden village of elves in an ancient tree
6. /imagine A haunted graveyard with wandering spirits
7. /imagine A grand wizard's tower filled with potions

8. /imagine A mythical sea monster rising from the ocean

9. /imagine A secret portal to another dimension

10. /imagine A heroic quest to retrieve a legendary sword

11. /imagine A whimsical tea party with talking animals

12. /imagine A frozen kingdom ruled by an ice queen

13. /imagine A steampunk city with mechanical inventions

14. /imagine A magical garden with singing flowers

15. /imagine A cursed pirate ship sailing ghostly seas

16. /imagine A grand ball in a fairy tale palace

17. /imagine A mystical oracle in a hidden cave

18. /imagine A flying carpet ride over a desert city

19. /imagine A battle of wits with a clever sphinx

20. /imagine A whimsical candy land with edible landscapes

21. /imagine A heroic rescue from a fire-breathing dragon

22. /imagine A magical transformation by a fairy godmother

23. /imagine A secret meeting of mythical creatures

24. /imagine A daring escape from a troll's

dungeon

25. /imagine A grand coronation of a fairy tale king

26. /imagine A mysterious encounter with a mermaid

27. /imagine A thrilling chase on broomsticks

28. /imagine A peaceful meditation with mystical monks

29. /imagine A grand feast in a dwarven hall

30. /imagine A magical duel between powerful sorcerers

31. /imagine A romantic dance under a moonlit waterfall

32. /imagine A thrilling adventure with a unicorn

33. /imagine A mysterious labyrinth with shifting walls

34. /imagine A peaceful village of hobbits in the hills

35. /imagine A grand cathedral with stained glass magic

36. /imagine A daring heist in a dragon's lair

37. /imagine A magical fountain of eternal youth

38. /imagine A whimsical circus with magical performers

39. /imagine A grand tournament of mythical beasts

40. /imagine A mysterious island floating in the sky

41. /imagine A magical harvest festival with

dancing scarecrows

42. /imagine A daring exploration of a sunken city
43. /imagine A grand parade of magical creatures
44. /imagine A mysterious forest path leading to a hidden world
45. /imagine A peaceful night's rest in a fairy's nest
46. /imagine A thrilling escape from a witch's curse
47. /imagine A grand library with knowledge of all magic
48. /imagine A mysterious moonlit ritual in a stone circle
49. /imagine A whimsical train ride to a magical school
50. /imagine A grand adventure with a band of heroic friends

These prompts offer a diverse exploration of fantasy worlds, capturing various magical landscapes, mythical creatures, whimsical adventures, and extraordinary experiences. Feel free to modify and experiment with these templates to create fantasy pieces that resonate with your imagination and sense of wonder. Happy creating!

17. PROMPT TEMPLATES FOR TECHNOLOGY AND INNOVATION

Technology and innovation are at the heart of human progress, shaping our lives and the world around us. This chapter provides 50 prompt templates to inspire and guide the creation of art that captures various technological themes, futuristic concepts, and innovative ideas.

1. /imagine A bustling futuristic cityscape with flying cars
2. /imagine A state-of-the-art robotics lab with humanoid robots
3. /imagine A virtual reality gaming experience in full immersion
4. /imagine A high-tech space station orbiting Earth
5. /imagine A cutting-edge medical procedure using nanotechnology
6. /imagine A renewable energy farm harnessing wind and solar power

7. /imagine A futuristic transportation hub with hyperloop trains

8. /imagine A smart home controlled by artificial intelligence

9. /imagine A high-tech factory with automated assembly lines

10. /imagine A futuristic classroom with holographic lessons

11. /imagine A cutting-edge biotechnology lab with genetic engineering

12. /imagine A virtual shopping mall with personalized avatars

13. /imagine A high-tech security system with facial recognition

14. /imagine A futuristic art studio with AI-assisted creativity

15. /imagine A cutting-edge wearable technology fashion show

16. /imagine A smart city with interconnected IoT devices

17. /imagine A high-tech agriculture farm with drone monitoring

18. /imagine A virtual concert with holographic musicians

19. /imagine A futuristic underwater research facility

20. /imagine A cutting-edge electric vehicle charging station

21. /imagine A high-tech recycling plant with zero waste

22. /imagine A futuristic battlefield with

    robotic soldiers

23. /imagine A cutting-edge 3D printing workshop

24. /imagine A smart fitness gym with AI personal trainers

25. /imagine A high-tech weather control station

26. /imagine A futuristic library with digital books

27. /imagine A cutting-edge quantum computing lab

28. /imagine A high-tech amusement park with VR rides

29. /imagine A futuristic bank with cryptocurrency transactions

30. /imagine A cutting-edge aerospace engineering facility

31. /imagine A high-tech emergency response center with drones

32. /imagine A futuristic restaurant with robotic chefs

33. /imagine A cutting-edge virtual courtroom

34. /imagine A high-tech wildlife conservation monitoring system

35. /imagine A futuristic space tourism launch pad

36. /imagine A cutting-edge augmented reality museum tour

37. /imagine A high-tech clean energy fusion reactor

38. /imagine A futuristic social media platform in virtual space
39. /imagine A cutting-edge prosthetics lab with bionic limbs
40. /imagine A high-tech autonomous delivery service
41. /imagine A futuristic ocean cleanup operation
42. /imagine A cutting-edge AI-driven stock market analysis
43. /imagine A high-tech smart grid for efficient energy distribution
44. /imagine A futuristic global internet satellite network
45. /imagine A cutting-edge brain-computer interface lab
46. /imagine A high-tech archaeological site with laser scanning
47. /imagine A futuristic climate change mitigation project
48. /imagine A cutting-edge eSports arena with interactive gaming
49. /imagine A high-tech disaster relief operation with AI coordination
50. /imagine A futuristic exploration of a distant exoplanet

These prompts offer a diverse exploration of technology and innovation, capturing various futuristic concepts, cutting-edge advancements, and technological wonders. Feel free to modify and experiment with these templates to create technological pieces that resonate with your curiosity and vision of the future. Happy creating!

18. PROMPT TEMPLATES FOR ANIMALS AND WILDLIFE

Animals and wildlife offer a rich source of inspiration, allowing us to explore the beauty, diversity, and complexity of the natural world. This chapter provides 50 prompt templates to inspire and guide the creation of art that captures various animal themes and wildlife scenarios.

1. /imagine A majestic lion roaring on a savanna
2. /imagine A playful dolphin leaping out of the ocean
3. /imagine A graceful deer in a misty forest
4. /imagine A colorful parrot chatting in a tropical jungle
5. /imagine A mysterious owl watching in the night
6. /imagine A lively meerkat family on the lookout
7. /imagine A powerful bear fishing in a

rushing river

8. /imagine A delicate butterfly landing on a flower
9. /imagine A wise elephant leading the herd
10. /imagine A speedy cheetah chasing its prey
11. /imagine A joyful kangaroo hopping in the outback
12. /imagine A fierce shark hunting in deep waters
13. /imagine A gentle panda munching on bamboo
14. /imagine A playful monkey swinging through trees
15. /imagine A regal peacock displaying its feathers
16. /imagine A loyal dog protecting its family
17. /imagine A curious cat exploring its surroundings
18. /imagine A graceful swan gliding on a lake
19. /imagine A busy bee collecting nectar
20. /imagine A stealthy fox hunting in the snow
21. /imagine A lively penguin family in the Antarctic
22. /imagine A mysterious bat flying in a cave
23. /imagine A colorful coral reef with diverse fish
24. /imagine A gentle giraffe grazing in the treetops
25. /imagine A powerful rhino charging in the wild

26. /imagine A playful otter sliding down a riverbank

27. /imagine A wise tortoise slowly exploring

28. /imagine A fierce eagle soaring in the mountains

29. /imagine A gentle manatee swimming in clear waters

30. /imagine A lively squirrel gathering nuts for winter

31. /imagine A mysterious octopus camouflaging in the sea

32. /imagine A graceful hummingbird hovering by a flower

33. /imagine A powerful wolf howling at the moon

34. /imagine A playful seal basking in the sun

35. /imagine A busy ant colony working together

36. /imagine A graceful gazelle leaping in the grasslands

37. /imagine A mysterious jaguar stalking in the jungle

38. /imagine A gentle sloth hanging from a branch

39. /imagine A lively frog jumping in a pond

40. /imagine A colorful chameleon changing its colors

41. /imagine A fierce crocodile lurking in the swamp

42. /imagine A gentle whale singing in the ocean

43. /imagine A lively raccoon exploring the city at night
44. /imagine A graceful falcon diving for its prey
45. /imagine A mysterious snow leopard in the Himalayas
46. /imagine A playful koala climbing eucalyptus trees
47. /imagine A powerful buffalo stampede on the plains
48. /imagine A gentle sea turtle nesting on the beach
49. /imagine A lively songbird serenading at dawn
50. /imagine A mysterious nocturnal aardvark digging

These prompts offer a diverse exploration of animals and wildlife, capturing various species, behaviors, habitats, and emotions. Feel free to modify and experiment with these templates to create animal-themed pieces that resonate with your appreciation for the natural world and its incredible inhabitants. Happy creating!

19. PROMPT TEMPLATES FOR FOOD AND CUISINE

Food and cuisine are universal languages that bring people together, celebrate culture, and satisfy our senses. This chapter provides 50 prompt templates to inspire and guide the creation of art that captures various culinary themes, delicious dishes, and gastronomic experiences.

1. /imagine A gourmet French dinner with escargot and coq au vin
2. /imagine A lively Italian pizzeria with wood-fired ovens
3. /imagine A traditional Japanese sushi bar with a master chef
4. /imagine A festive Mexican taco stand with colorful decorations
5. /imagine A bustling Chinese dim sum restaurant with carts
6. /imagine A cozy British tea time with scones and jam
7. /imagine A lively American barbecue with grills and smokers

8. /imagine A traditional Indian curry feast with naan bread
9. /imagine A romantic candlelit dinner with wine and dessert
10. /imagine A festive German beer garden with pretzels
11. /imagine A bustling Spanish tapas bar with sangria
12. /imagine A lively Brazilian churrascaria with skewers
13. /imagine A traditional Moroccan tagine meal with spices
14. /imagine A gourmet seafood platter with lobster and oysters
15. /imagine A festive Hawaiian luau with a pig roast
16. /imagine A traditional Korean barbecue with tabletop grills
17. /imagine A bustling Thai street food market with pad thai
18. /imagine A gourmet chocolate tasting with various flavors
19. /imagine A lively Greek taverna with moussaka and dancing
20. /imagine A traditional Ethiopian meal with injera bread
21. /imagine A festive Mardi Gras feast with gumbo and beignets
22. /imagine A gourmet farm-to-table meal with fresh ingredients
23. /imagine A bustling Vietnamese pho

restaurant with herbs

24. /imagine A lively Turkish kebab house with grilled meats

25. /imagine A traditional Russian meal with borscht and caviar

26. /imagine A gourmet wine and cheese pairing experience

27. /imagine A lively Cuban sandwich shop with music

28. /imagine A traditional Jewish Passover Seder meal

29. /imagine A gourmet vegan feast with colorful vegetables

30. /imagine A bustling Belgian waffle house with toppings

31. /imagine A lively Peruvian ceviche bar with citrus

32. /imagine A traditional Swedish smorgasbord with herring

33. /imagine A gourmet cake decorating workshop

34. /imagine A lively Canadian poutine truck with gravy

35. /imagine A traditional Middle Eastern falafel stand

36. /imagine A gourmet coffee tasting with various brews

37. /imagine A lively Irish pub with stew and beer

38. /imagine A traditional Filipino lechon roast celebration

39. /imagine A gourmet ice cream parlor with unique flavors
40. /imagine A bustling Australian meat pie shop
41. /imagine A lively South African braai barbecue
42. /imagine A traditional Polish pierogi feast with family
43. /imagine A gourmet tea ceremony with artisanal blends
44. /imagine A lively New York deli with sandwiches
45. /imagine A traditional Swiss fondue meal with friends
46. /imagine A gourmet molecular gastronomy tasting menu
47. /imagine A lively Argentinian asado barbecue with chimichurri
48. /imagine A traditional Dutch pancake house with toppings
49. /imagine A gourmet farm-fresh breakfast with eggs and bacon
50. /imagine A lively Jamaican jerk chicken stand with spices

These prompts offer a diverse exploration of food and cuisine, capturing various culinary traditions, delicious dishes, dining experiences, and gastronomic delights. Feel free to modify and experiment with these templates to create food-themed pieces that resonate with your appreciation for the art of cooking and the joy of eating. Happy creating!

20. PROMPT TEMPLATES FOR FASHION AND STYLE

Fashion and style are expressive mediums that reflect individuality, culture, and creativity. This chapter provides 50 prompt templates to inspire and guide the creation of art that captures various fashion themes, clothing designs, accessories, and style trends.

1. /imagine A glamorous runway show during Fashion Week
2. /imagine A chic Parisian street style with berets and scarves
3. /imagine A traditional Japanese kimono with intricate patterns
4. /imagine A lively hip-hop street dance with urban wear
5. /imagine A sophisticated black-tie event with elegant gowns
6. /imagine A rugged cowboy look with boots and hats
7. /imagine A futuristic fashion line with tech-inspired designs

8. /imagine A colorful tropical beachwear collection
9. /imagine A traditional Indian wedding attire with jewelry
10. /imagine A punk rock concert with leather and spikes
11. /imagine A cozy winter look with knit sweaters and scarves
12. /imagine A lively carnival costume with feathers and sequins
13. /imagine A chic office look with tailored suits and briefcases
14. /imagine A retro 1950s diner look with poodle skirts
15. /imagine A sustainable eco-friendly fashion line
16. /imagine A glamorous Hollywood red carpet event
17. /imagine A lively African tribal dance with traditional wear
18. /imagine A chic urban streetwear collection with graffiti
19. /imagine A romantic Victorian era look with corsets
20. /imagine A futuristic space-themed fashion line
21. /imagine A traditional Scottish kilt with bagpipes
22. /imagine A lively salsa dance with colorful dresses
23. /imagine A chic minimalist fashion line

with neutral tones

24. /imagine A rugged outdoor adventure look with hiking gear
25. /imagine A glamorous vintage Hollywood starlet look
26. /imagine A lively children's fashion show with playful designs
27. /imagine A chic bridal fashion show with elegant gowns
28. /imagine A traditional Chinese New Year celebration attire
29. /imagine A lively hipster look with beards and tattoos
30. /imagine A sophisticated jazz club look with fedoras
31. /imagine A rugged military-inspired fashion line
32. /imagine A lively fitness workout look with activewear
33. /imagine A chic fashion blogger's daily outfit
34. /imagine A traditional Middle Eastern belly dance attire
35. /imagine A glamorous masquerade ball with masks
36. /imagine A lively rockabilly dance with vintage wear
37. /imagine A chic fashion photographer's studio
38. /imagine A traditional Native American powwow attire

39. /imagine A lively fashion design workshop with sketches
40. /imagine A glamorous fashion magazine cover shoot
41. /imagine A traditional Greek folk dance with costumes
42. /imagine A lively fashion school classroom with students
43. /imagine A chic fashion influencer's social media post
44. /imagine A traditional Nordic Viking attire with fur
45. /imagine A lively fashion retail store with shoppers
46. /imagine A chic fashion model's backstage preparation
47. /imagine A traditional Maori dance with tribal tattoos
48. /imagine A lively fashion collaboration brainstorming session
49. /imagine A chic fashion editor's office with mood boards
50. /imagine A glamorous fashion awards ceremony with celebrities

These prompts offer a diverse exploration of fashion and style, capturing various clothing designs, fashion trends, cultural attire, and style expressions. Feel free to modify and experiment with these templates to create fashion-themed pieces that resonate with your appreciation for the art of clothing design and the beauty of personal style. Happy creating!

21. PROMPT TEMPLATES FOR SPORTS AND ACTIVITIES

Sports and activities are a vibrant part of human culture, offering excitement, competition, teamwork, and personal growth. This chapter provides 50 prompt templates to inspire and guide the creation of art that captures various sports, games, physical activities, and athletic themes.

1. /imagine A thrilling soccer match in a packed stadium
2. /imagine A graceful ballet performance on stage
3. /imagine A high-energy basketball game with slam dunks
4. /imagine A serene yoga session at sunrise
5. /imagine A fierce boxing match in a roaring arena
6. /imagine A lively beach volleyball game with friends
7. /imagine A thrilling downhill skiing race

on snowy slopes

8. /imagine A peaceful fishing trip on a calm lake

9. /imagine A high-stakes poker game in a casino

10. /imagine A challenging rock climbing adventure

11. /imagine A lively street basketball game with tricks

12. /imagine A graceful figure skating performance

13. /imagine A thrilling motocross race on a dirt track

14. /imagine A peaceful tai chi practice in a garden

15. /imagine A high-energy dance battle in a club

16. /imagine A thrilling Formula 1 race with speed

17. /imagine A challenging marathon race with cheering crowds

18. /imagine A lively family picnic with games

19. /imagine A thrilling surfing ride on a big wave

20. /imagine A peaceful meditation session in nature

21. /imagine A high-energy Zumba class with music

22. /imagine A thrilling skydiving jump from a plane

23. /imagine A peaceful golf game on a scenic

course

24. /imagine A lively skateboarding session at a park

25. /imagine A thrilling mountain biking adventure

26. /imagine A graceful gymnastics routine on the floor

27. /imagine A lively roller derby match with action

28. /imagine A thrilling whitewater rafting adventure

29. /imagine A peaceful archery practice with focus

30. /imagine A high-energy CrossFit workout in a gym

31. /imagine A thrilling hockey game with fast action

32. /imagine A peaceful sailing trip on the ocean

33. /imagine A lively ping pong match with friends

34. /imagine A thrilling snowboarding ride on fresh powder

35. /imagine A graceful synchronized swimming performance

36. /imagine A thrilling bull riding event at a rodeo

37. /imagine A peaceful bird watching expedition

38. /imagine A lively dodgeball game with excitement

39. /imagine A thrilling BMX biking stunt show
40. /imagine A graceful ballroom dancing competition
41. /imagine A thrilling triathlon race with endurance
42. /imagine A peaceful kite flying session on a windy day
43. /imagine A lively fencing duel with precision
44. /imagine A thrilling paragliding flight over mountains
45. /imagine A graceful cheerleading routine at a game
46. /imagine A thrilling scuba diving exploration of a reef
47. /imagine A peaceful tai chi practice in a park
48. /imagine A lively carnival game booth with prizes
49. /imagine A thrilling hang gliding adventure over valleys
50. /imagine A graceful aerial silk performance in a circus

These prompts offer a diverse exploration of sports and activities, capturing various physical pursuits, competitive games, recreational hobbies, and athletic performances. Feel free to modify and experiment with these templates to create sports-themed pieces that resonate with your appreciation for the energy, grace, excitement, and camaraderie found in the world of sports and physical activities. Happy creating!

22. PROMPT TEMPLATES FOR VEHICLES AND TRANSPORTATION

Vehicles and transportation are essential aspects of modern life, connecting people, places, and cultures. This chapter provides 50 prompt templates to inspire and guide the creation of art that captures various modes of transportation, vehicle designs, travel experiences, and technological advancements.

1. /imagine A bustling city street with taxis and buses
2. /imagine A high-speed bullet train racing through the countryside
3. /imagine A vintage car show with classic models
4. /imagine A futuristic spaceport with interstellar travel
5. /imagine A lively bicycle race through scenic landscapes
6. /imagine A peaceful sailboat journey on a

calm sea

7. /imagine A thrilling motorcycle ride on a winding road

8. /imagine A bustling airport terminal with travelers

9. /imagine A vintage steam locomotive chugging through mountains

10. /imagine A futuristic self-driving car in a smart city

11. /imagine A lively skateboard park with tricks and jumps

12. /imagine A peaceful hot air balloon ride over vineyards

13. /imagine A thrilling fighter jet maneuvering in the sky

14. /imagine A bustling subway station during rush hour

15. /imagine A vintage Vespa ride through Italian streets

16. /imagine A futuristic hyperloop station with sleek pods

17. /imagine A lively ATV adventure on rugged trails

18. /imagine A peaceful gondola ride in Venice canals

19. /imagine A thrilling drag race with powerful cars

20. /imagine A bustling seaport with cargo ships

21. /imagine A lively snowmobile ride in a winter wonderland

22. /imagine A peaceful horse-drawn carriage in a historic town
23. /imagine A thrilling helicopter tour over a city skyline
24. /imagine A vintage tram ride through San Francisco
25. /imagine A futuristic electric vehicle charging station
26. /imagine A lively scooter ride through narrow alleys
27. /imagine A peaceful kayak journey on a tranquil river
28. /imagine A thrilling monster truck rally in a stadium
29. /imagine A bustling rickshaw ride in a crowded market
30. /imagine A vintage biplane flying over farmlands
31. /imagine A futuristic flying car in an urban landscape
32. /imagine A lively rollerblading session on a beach boardwalk
33. /imagine A peaceful cruise ship sailing into the sunset
34. /imagine A thrilling jet ski ride on choppy waves
35. /imagine A bustling tuk-tuk ride in a Thai street
36. /imagine A vintage Route 66 road trip with classic cars
37. /imagine A futuristic space shuttle launch

at a space center

38. /imagine A lively BMX biking session in a skate park

39. /imagine A peaceful glider flight over scenic hills

40. /imagine A bustling bus terminal with diverse passengers

41. /imagine A lively Segway tour through a city park

42. /imagine A peaceful canoe trip in a forest lake

43. /imagine A thrilling Formula E electric car race

44. /imagine A vintage ferry ride with scenic views

45. /imagine A futuristic robotic delivery drone in action

46. /imagine A lively amusement park train ride

47. /imagine A peaceful longboard ride on a coastal road

48. /imagine A bustling motorcycle taxi ride in a busy city

49. /imagine A vintage cable car ride in a mountain resort

50. /imagine A futuristic autonomous cargo ship at sea

These prompts offer a diverse exploration of vehicles and transportation, capturing various modes of travel, vehicle designs, transportation experiences, and technological innovations. Feel free to modify and experiment with these templates to create transportation-themed pieces that resonate with your appreciation for the movement, connection, and technological advancements found in the world of vehicles and travel. Happy creating!

23. PROMPT TEMPLATES FOR ARCHITECTURE AND BUILDINGS

Architecture and buildings are a testament to human creativity, innovation, and cultural expression. This chapter provides 50 prompt templates to inspire and guide the creation of art that captures various architectural styles, iconic buildings, urban landscapes, and interior spaces.

1. /imagine A bustling New York City skyline with iconic skyscrapers
2. /imagine A serene Japanese Zen garden with traditional architecture
3. /imagine A futuristic cityscape with innovative buildings
4. /imagine A historic European castle with intricate details
5. /imagine A lively urban street with cafes and shops
6. /imagine A peaceful countryside cottage with a garden

7. /imagine A thrilling futuristic space colony on Mars

8. /imagine A vintage Victorian mansion with ornate decor

9. /imagine A bustling modern airport terminal with travelers

10. /imagine A serene beachfront bungalow with ocean views

11. /imagine A lively college campus with students and activities

12. /imagine A peaceful monastery in the Himalayan mountains

13. /imagine A bustling shopping mall with diverse stores

14. /imagine A historic Roman Colosseum with gladiators

15. /imagine A futuristic underwater city with domes

16. /imagine A lively amusement park with colorful attractions

17. /imagine A peaceful treehouse in a lush forest

18. /imagine A bustling industrial factory with machinery

19. /imagine A historic Egyptian pyramid with hieroglyphics

20. /imagine A futuristic smart home with automation

21. /imagine A lively downtown square with a fountain

22. /imagine A peaceful desert oasis with palm

trees

23. /imagine A thrilling futuristic space station orbiting Earth

24. /imagine A vintage 1950s diner with neon signs

25. /imagine A bustling construction site with cranes

26. /imagine A serene mountain cabin with a fireplace

27. /imagine A lively sports stadium with cheering fans

28. /imagine A peaceful Buddhist temple with monks

29. /imagine A bustling train station with commuters

30. /imagine A historic Gothic cathedral with stained glass

31. /imagine A futuristic eco-friendly city with green roofs

32. /imagine A lively urban park with families and activities

33. /imagine A peaceful spa retreat with natural elements

34. /imagine A bustling harbor with boats and docks

35. /imagine A historic Wild West town with saloons

36. /imagine A futuristic virtual reality gaming arena

37. /imagine A lively schoolyard with children playing

38. /imagine A peaceful greenhouse with exotic plants
39. /imagine A bustling farmers' market with fresh produce
40. /imagine A historic lighthouse on a rocky shore
41. /imagine A futuristic floating city on the ocean
42. /imagine A lively art studio with creative works
43. /imagine A peaceful library with endless shelves
44. /imagine A bustling hotel lobby with guests
45. /imagine A historic Great Wall of China with watchtowers
46. /imagine A futuristic robotic manufacturing facility
47. /imagine A lively casino floor with games and lights
48. /imagine A peaceful yoga studio with natural light
49. /imagine A bustling subway tunnel with graffiti
50. /imagine A historic Greek Parthenon with columns

These prompts offer a diverse exploration of architecture and buildings, capturing various architectural styles, iconic structures, urban landscapes, and interior spaces. Feel free to modify and experiment with these templates to create architecture-themed pieces that resonate with your appreciation for the design, history, innovation, and cultural significance found in the world of architecture and construction. Happy creating!

24. PROMPT TEMPLATES FOR HEALTH AND WELLNESS

Health and wellness encompass a broad range of topics, including physical fitness, mental well-being, nutrition, medical care, and holistic practices. This chapter provides 50 prompt templates to inspire and guide the creation of art that captures various aspects of health, healing, self-care, and wellness.

1. /imagine A serene meditation session with calming candles
2. /imagine A lively fitness class with energetic participants
3. /imagine A peaceful acupuncture treatment with soothing music
4. /imagine A bustling farmer's market with fresh produce
5. /imagine A tranquil spa retreat with natural therapies
6. /imagine A lively children's playground with laughter

7. /imagine A peaceful therapy session with a compassionate counselor
8. /imagine A bustling hospital ward with dedicated nurses
9. /imagine A serene yoga practice on a mountain top
10. /imagine A futuristic medical lab with advanced technology
11. /imagine A lively community garden with blooming flowers
12. /imagine A peaceful home-cooked meal with family
13. /imagine A tranquil forest hike with fresh air
14. /imagine A bustling gym with various workout equipment
15. /imagine A serene herbal tea ceremony with healing herbs
16. /imagine A peaceful beach walk with gentle waves
17. /imagine A lively dance therapy session with joyful movement
18. /imagine A tranquil massage therapy room with aromatherapy
19. /imagine A bustling nutritionist's office with healthy plans
20. /imagine A peaceful mindfulness retreat with nature
21. /imagine A lively school cafeteria with nutritious meals
22. /imagine A tranquil birthing center with

supportive care

23. /imagine A futuristic wellness center with holistic treatments
24. /imagine A peaceful bedroom with restful sleep
25. /imagine A bustling rehabilitation center with recovery
26. /imagine A serene Tai Chi practice in a garden
27. /imagine A peaceful therapy animal visit with smiles
28. /imagine A lively neighborhood walk with friends
29. /imagine A tranquil aromatherapy session with essential oils
30. /imagine A bustling dental clinic with bright smiles
31. /imagine A peaceful reading nook with inspiring books
32. /imagine A lively family bike ride on a sunny day
33. /imagine A tranquil sound therapy session with singing bowls
34. /imagine A bustling community health fair with education
35. /imagine A peaceful art therapy studio with creativity
36. /imagine A lively senior center with engaging activities
37. /imagine A tranquil reiki healing session with energy

38. /imagine A bustling pharmacy with helpful medications
39. /imagine A peaceful home garden with healing plants
40. /imagine A lively support group meeting with empathy
41. /imagine A tranquil lakeside fishing trip with relaxation
42. /imagine A bustling pediatrician's office with care
43. /imagine A peaceful journaling session with self-reflection
44. /imagine A lively outdoor picnic with wholesome food
45. /imagine A tranquil chiropractic adjustment with alignment
46. /imagine A bustling mental health clinic with support
47. /imagine A peaceful prenatal yoga class with mothers
48. /imagine A lively cooking class with healthy recipes
49. /imagine A tranquil therapy garden with sensory experiences
50. /imagine A futuristic telemedicine consultation with convenience

These prompts offer a diverse exploration of health and wellness, capturing various aspects of physical health, mental well-being, holistic practices, medical care, and self-care activities. Feel free to modify and experiment with these templates to create health-themed pieces that resonate with your appreciation for the balance, healing, vitality, and nurturing found in the world of health and wellness. Happy creating!

25. PROMPT TEMPLATES FOR EDUCATION AND LEARNING

Education and learning are vital aspects of personal growth, societal development, and cultural enrichment. This chapter provides 50 prompt templates to inspire and guide the creation of art that captures various educational settings, learning experiences, academic subjects, and educational innovations.

1. /imagine A lively elementary school classroom with eager students
2. /imagine A peaceful library with endless shelves of knowledge
3. /imagine A bustling university campus with diverse learners
4. /imagine A futuristic virtual reality classroom with immersion
5. /imagine A serene art studio with creative expression
6. /imagine A lively science lab with exciting

experiments

7. /imagine A peaceful study nook with focused concentration

8. /imagine A bustling online learning platform with global access

9. /imagine A serene music room with harmonious melodies

10. /imagine A lively debate competition with persuasive arguments

11. /imagine A peaceful outdoor classroom with nature

12. /imagine A bustling vocational workshop with hands-on skills

13. /imagine A serene reading circle with engaging storytelling

14. /imagine A lively mathematics class with problem-solving

15. /imagine A peaceful meditation session for mindfulness in education

16. /imagine A bustling educational technology conference

17. /imagine A serene writing workshop with inspired authors

18. /imagine A lively school assembly with student achievements

19. /imagine A peaceful historical museum with artifacts

20. /imagine A bustling coding bootcamp with innovative projects

21. /imagine A serene language immersion class with cultural exchange

22. /imagine A lively school cafeteria with social interactions
23. /imagine A peaceful study abroad experience with exploration
24. /imagine A bustling teacher's lounge with collaboration
25. /imagine A serene school garden with environmental learning
26. /imagine A lively gym class with physical education
27. /imagine A peaceful tutoring session with personalized support
28. /imagine A bustling school bus with cheerful students
29. /imagine A serene astronomy observatory with stargazing
30. /imagine A lively school theater with dramatic performances
31. /imagine A peaceful adult education class with lifelong learning
32. /imagine A bustling robotics competition with innovation
33. /imagine A serene geography class with world exploration
34. /imagine A lively school fair with community engagement
35. /imagine A peaceful philosophy seminar with deep discussions
36. /imagine A bustling school library with young readers
37. /imagine A serene online tutoring session

with a helpful mentor

38. /imagine A lively school sports day with teamwork

39. /imagine A peaceful poetry reading with literary appreciation

40. /imagine A bustling makerspace with creative inventions

41. /imagine A serene school counseling office with support

42. /imagine A lively history class with time-traveling adventures

43. /imagine A peaceful biology greenhouse with plant studies

44. /imagine A lively school dance with joyful celebration

45. /imagine A peaceful night school with dedicated learners

46. /imagine A bustling educational field trip with discovery

47. /imagine A serene school art gallery with student creations

48. /imagine A lively school science fair with young inventors

49. /imagine A peaceful school choir practice with harmony

50. /imagine A futuristic AI-driven personalized learning platform

These prompts offer a diverse exploration of education and learning, capturing various educational environments, learning experiences, academic subjects, and innovative educational practices. Feel free to modify and experiment with these templates to create education-themed pieces that resonate with your appreciation for the growth, discovery, creativity, and empowerment found in the world of education and learning. Happy creating!

CONCLUSION

The journey through "MidJourney Mastery" has been an exploration of creativity, innovation, and the limitless potential of human imagination. From the foundational understanding of MidJourney commands to the diverse and inspiring prompt templates across various themes, this book has aimed to be a comprehensive guide for artists, creators, and enthusiasts alike.

The 1000+ prompt templates provided in this book are not just a set of instructions but an invitation to explore, experiment, and express. They are a starting point for your unique creations, whether you're a seasoned artist or just beginning your creative journey.

The world of MidJourney is ever-evolving, and so is the landscape of art and creativity. The templates and insights shared in this book are meant to be timeless yet adaptable, allowing you to infuse your personal touch, cultural context, and innovative ideas.

Remember, creativity is not confined to rules or boundaries. It thrives on curiosity, courage, and collaboration. May this book serve as a catalyst for your creative endeavors, inspiring you to push the boundaries of conventional art and embrace the exciting possibilities of MidJourney.

Thank you for embarking on this journey with us. The path to mastery is endless, filled with learning, growth, and endless inspiration. Keep exploring, keep creating, and most importantly, enjoy the journey.

Happy creating!